WELCOME WORDS FROM JF BROU

Hi, I'm Jean-Francois. Like most of you, my financial life dimensions have always been messy. Do you know anyone in your circle that has never struggled with money? Roughly none, right! Well, it's normal because the current education system is not teaching us how to manage and make money. On top of that, we are incentivized to spend more and take debt. None of the chapters of this workbook are taught in school, which is so sad.

So, to begin with, don't blame yourself; you are normal. Secondly, be proud of yourself because you are now taking massive action on your financial situation by doing this workbook. I'm giving you the best content and strategies available out there.

I've spent years trying to fix my financial problems. As a creative entrepreneur, throughout my career, I've been very driven and found ways to sell my products. But even after millions of dollars in sales, I always ended up broke, until I finally found the right strategy.

Everything is energy, and like all of us, I had a lot of money wounds and abundance blocks stopping the natural flow of energy. All those blockages were embedded from my parents and my environment in the first 7 years of my life. I had to release those trapped energies to become an abundant being.

Once you start working with energies, you can fix anything in your life. Because, yes, we attract what we are. We attract the frequencies we emit.

THE STORY BEHIND WHY I CREATED THIS WORKBOOK

I created this workbook for my brother who is stuck with the same condition as me, my family so they can understand why I act in different ways, my girlfriend, my future children and my fellow Self-Explorers. I wanted to do something simple, action driven step by step, so we can all live in abundance. Because once each individual reaches financial stability, they stop worrying and start thinking about how to help others, and how to live with passion.

Another truth is that I created this workbook for myself first. I couldn't live with my financial problems anymore. They were ruining all my other life dimensions, keeping me inside my head constantly worrying about how to pay this supplier, employees, bills, etc.

I always wanted to become the best version of myself, as most of you know from my first workbook of this *Become Series, Become Your Best Version.* But I couldn't ever become my best version without living on the abundance frequency.

HOW TO USE THIS WORKBOOK

This is an intense workbook. Yes, it can be overwhelming depending on where you are in your journey, but make sure not to be too hard on yourself, as everyone is different. I highly recommend blocking 4 sessions of 2 hours in the next 10 days. You can also share the workbook or your answers for each chapter with a friend or family member to be fully accountable. The more you engage in discussion about those topics, the more it will help you understand the depth of the content. You might get stuck on some exercises, which is ok. Expand your research on the Internet with the resources and let it rest for a little while.

WHAT DOES IT MEAN TO BECOME FINANCIALLY FREE?

Becoming financially free is not a promise to become rich like all the rags to-riches advertisements you might see out there. You might even most likely not become a millionaire. Becoming financially free means that your money problems and habits don't control you anymore. It means to live out of debt. It means to be satisfied with what you have. It means you can work with passion helping others instead of working to make money. It means you could stop working for 1-2 years and still continue to make money and live a good lifestyle.

SO, ARE YOU READY TO LIVE A LIFE
OF ABUNDANCE AND PURPOSE?

Money Personality

CHAPTER 1 :

1 hour & 30 minutes to complete

"IF YOU DON'T KNOW WHO YOU TRULY ARE, YOU'LL NEVER KNOW WHAT YOU REALLY WANT."

~ ROY T. BENNETT

We are starting strong here, you'll realize. Doing these personality tests below will make you realize your money type, attitude and patterns. It will lead you to ask yourself why and how you became this way or another. Have fun discovering yourself.

1.1. WHAT IS YOUR MONEY EQ TYPE?

This exercise comes with the free Mindvalley master class: The Japanese Art of Healing Your Money Wounds with Ken Honda.

Ken Honda is introduced as a self-help author superstar in Japan, but is not widely known in the Eastern world. Through the master class, he explains how money EQ, your emotional decisions around money, is more important than money IQ, your knowledge around making and managing money.

HERE'S THE QUIZ TO KNOW YOUR TYPE. RATE THE AFFIRMATIONS BELOW FROM 1 TO 5:

1 is *I strongly disagree*
2 is *I disagree*
3 is I am *neutral*
4 is I *agree*
5 is I *strongly agree*

MONEY EQ QUIZ		RESULT
1	I spend a lot of time thinking about what I will do with my money. Save it, earn it, spend it	
2	I would like more money in my life and have many plans for what I would do with it	
3	I am happier when I am actively doing something to change my finances	
4	Money seems to flow easily to me without efforts	
5	I don't spend much time thinking about money	
6	I am generally not very motivated by money	
7	I spend a lot of time worrying about money	
8	I often find myself frozen when it comes to making financial decisions	
9	I will often ignore my finances or keep money at a distance	

MONEY EQ RESULTS	TOTAL
Add up your results for questions 1, 2, 3	
Add up your results for questions 4, 5, 6	
Add up your results for questions 7, 8, 9	

RESULTS, circle whichever type you scored a high rating on (you might have more than one type).

Questions 1, 2, 3 = Controlling type
Questions 4, 5, 6 = Indifferent type
Questions 7, 8, 9 = Fearful type

There are three money EQ (Emotional Intelligence) types:

1. CONTROLLING
   Rigid like Ice. The controlling type manipulates, does things to make more and could sell anything. He is cheap, he is making money to avoid his inner pain and have a mindset of "if I had more I would be happier".

2. INDIFFERENT
   Flowing like water. The indifferent type is comfortable around money; he doesn't have to worry about it because he was raised in a good environment. They most likely become teachers or social workers.

3. FEARFUL
   Evaporates like air. The fearful type has a hippie mindset. He thinks that money is bad and evil. He's careless, worries about paying bills, and runs away from money when he makes some.

How you think you fit perfectly in your main types:

Take notes on your new awareness about your type and your parents' relations with money when you were a child or even your whole environment around money as a child:

1.2. MONEY HARMONY QUIZ

This quiz is taken from Chapter One of *Money Harmony: A Road Map for Individuals and Couples*, by Olivia Mellan and Sherry Christie.

TAKE THE QUIZ HERE TO GET YOUR RESULTS:
https://www.moneyharmony.com/moneyharmony-quiz

MONEY HARMONY RESULTS	RESULT
Amasser	
Avoider	
Spender	
Money Monk	
Hoarder	

Here are the 5 money harmony types:

AMASSER

If you tend to be a money amasser, you are happiest when you have large amounts of money at your disposal to spend, to save, and/or to invest. If you are not actually spending, saving, or investing, you may feel empty or not fully alive. You tend to equate money with self-worth and power, so a lack of money may lead to feelings of failure and even depression.

If you hire an investment advisor or financial planner, your major concern will be finding investments with high rates of return, since you hope to make as much money as you can, as quickly as possible. You probably enjoy making your own financial decisions, so it may be quite difficult for you to give up much control to money professionals.

If, on the other hand, you tend to be a worrier, too, and if you are tired of being overly obsessed with your money, you may actually welcome the opportunity to assign some of the details of your money life to a trustworthy financial advisor.

AVOIDER

If you tend to be a money avoider, you probably have a hard time balancing your checkbook, paying your bills promptly, and doing your taxes until the very last minute. You may avoid making a budget or keeping any kind of financial record. You won't know how much money you have, how much you owe, or how much you spend.

You may avoid investing money, even if you do have some, because it seems like too much trouble to attend to such details. What fuels this avoidance? You may feel incompetent or overwhelmed when faced with the tasks of your money life. If you are an extreme money avoider, you may even feel a kind of money anxiety or paralysis when faced with money tasks that resemble the feelings associated with math anxiety.

Some money avoiders share with money monks the belief that money is dirty. Others have a kind of aristocratic disdain toward the boring, seemingly unimportant details of their money life. But most avoiders are more prone to feeling that they are inadequate or incompetent in dealing with the complexities and the details of their money life, rather than feeling they are above such dirty work.

HOARDER

If you tend to be a hoarder, you like to save money. You also like to prioritize your financial goals. You probably have a budget and may enjoy the processes of making up a budget and reviewing it periodically. You most likely have a hard time spending money on yourself and your loved ones for luxury items or even practical gifts. These purchases would seem frivolous to you. You might very well view spending money on entertainment and vacations - and even on clothing - as largely unnecessary expenses.

If you think about investing your money, you tend to be concerned not with liquidity, but with future security, especially during retirement. "Saving for a rainy day" appeals to your orderly nature. If you are an extreme hoarder, you may want to keep your money so close to you that you avoid putting it even in conservative investments such as money markets, bonds, or mutual funds.

Some hoarders have been known to keep their money hidden under mattresses and in other secret places rather than put it in a bank. However, these cases are relatively rare. Depending on how extreme your hoarder tendencies are, you might exhibit some, most, or all of these traits.

MONEY MONK

If you are a money monk, you think that money is dirty, that it is bad, and that if you have too much of it, it will corrupt you. In general, you believe that "money is the root of all evil." It stands to reason that you identify with people of modest means rather than with those who amass wealth.

If you happen to come into a windfall somehow (through inheritance, for example), you will tend to be uneasy and even very anxious at the thought of the influx of so much money. You'd worry that you might "sell out," becoming greedier and more selfish, and losing sight of positive human, political, and/or spiritual ideals and values.

You would probably avoid investing your money, for fear that it might grow and make you even wealthier. If you were willing to invest some of it, you would most likely be comfortable only with socially responsible investments that reflected your deeper values and convictions and that contributed to causes you would like to support.

SPENDER

If you are a spender, you enjoy using your money to buy yourself goods and services for your immediate pleasure. You probably get satisfaction from spending money on gifts for others. The odds are that you have a hard time saving money and prioritizing the things you'd like in your life. As a result, it may be difficult for you to put aside enough money for future-oriented purchases and long-term financial goals.

You may spend most or all of the money you earn, and you may even be in debt. Now, it is important to realize that some people who are in debt are not spenders; they may simply not make enough money to meet their basic needs. If your own income is insufficient to meet your expenses, you are facing a real money crisis. You will have to come up with strategies to generate more income.

Key characteristics of your main type:

Take notes on your new awareness about your type and your parents' relations with money when you were a child or even your whole environment around money as a child:

1.3. MONEY BELIEF TYPE

TAKE THE QUIZ HERE:
https://www.nerdwallet.com/blog/finance/money-personalities-which-one-describes-you/

A **score of 8 and above** indicates that you strongly hold this belief.

MONEY BELIEF RESULTS	RESULT
Money Worship	
Money Avoidance	
Money Vigilance	
Money Statues	

Here's the explanation of each type.

MONEY WORSHIP

Money worshippers believe that more money will solve their problems and they can never have enough money. They are more likely to overspend on themselves or others and carry credit card debt. Money worship is the most common belief among Americans, according to research by Klontz.

Take action: If you're a money worshipper, you can take control of your spending by creating a budget and learning about the different ways to pay off credit card debt.

MONEY AVOIDANCE

Avoiders believe that money is bad and they do not deserve it. They may ignore their finances and avoid thinking about money. They may also give away money to others in order not to have it.

Take action: One option, if you're an avoider, is to automate your finances to avoid thinking about them—setting up automatic 401(k) contributions or sending money to a separate savings account, for example. Loved ones can help hold you accountable to those tasks.

MONEY VIGILANCE

Those who are vigilant believe that being frugal and saving is important. They may be secretive about their finances and uncomfortable discussing money with others.

Take action: Secrecy should not stand in the way of better money habits. If you're uncomfortable talking to family or friends but have money questions, use NerdWallet to find the best savings accounts for an emergency fund, research investment options, or get the right credit card to match your spending habits.

MONEY STATUS

People who hold this belief see money as a means to achieving a higher status. They believe self-worth is equal to net worth and may be driven to earn more money than their peers. They may also take risks to make money quickly and buy expensive things.

Take action: If you hold this belief, give yourself a cooling-off period before making a purchase. You can also make a budget—and stick to it—to avoid overspending.

Key characteristics of your main type:

Take notes on your new awareness about your type and your parents' relations with money when you were a child or even your whole environment around money as a child:

CHAPTER 2 :

20 minutes to complete

Limited Beliefs

"THE SKY IS NOT THE LIMIT.
YOUR BELIEF SYSTEM IS."

~ UNKNOWN

Our subconscious mind is built from the age 0 to 7 where our brain lives in a constant theta waves state. Theta waves are the most imprintable; we absorb everything in our environment. It's also the waves reached by a high level of meditation. After the age of 7, we live 95% of our days from our subconscious mind, so what we imprint in the early age is what we are. The only way to get rid of the things you don't want any more is through repetition through affirmations and habits and hypnosis.

2.1. SELF-LIMITING BELIEFS QUESTION

Taken from this FREE master class:
The Japanese Art of Healing Your Money Wounds Masterclass with Ken Honda.

RATE THE AFFIRMATIONS BELOW FROM 1 TO 5

1 is *I strongly disagree*
2 is *I disagree*
3 is I am *neutral*
4 is I *agree*
5 is I *strongly agree*

	SELF-LIMITING BELIEFS QUESTION QUIZ	RESULT
1	If I got rich, I would lose the people around me	
2	If I got rich, I wouldn't be able to trust anyone	
3	If I got wealthy, I would have to sacrifice my wealth, health, and/or friendship to get there	
4	If I got wealthy, I would be less spiritual	
5	If I got wealthy, I would have to compromise some of my values	
6	To get wealthy, it requires hard work	
7	With wealth comes greed, selfishness, and arrogance	

Circle two beliefs from the above that you want to work on and turn them into positive affirmations below you'll repeat to yourself daily

1 ....

2 ....

2.2. MORE LIMITED BELIEFS AFFIRMATIONS

Underline your top 5 limited beliefs below that you want to work on in the next few months.

1. *Money is the root of all evil.*
2. *Money is not that important. It's only money.*
3. *Money is there to be spent.*
4. *The rich get richer, while the poor get poorer.*
5. *I'm just not good with money.*
6. *My family has never been rich.*
7. *Money is a limited resource.*
8. *You have to work (too) hard to get wealthy.*
9. *It's selfish to want a lot of money.*
10. *Everything needs to happen today.*
11. *It takes money to make money.*
12. *I can't live a balanced life if I want to make a lot of money.*
13. *My financial success depends on the job market and the economy.*
14. *To make money, you must take big risks.*
15. *Money is the measure of my success and/or worth.*
16. *Life is hard.*
17. *Most wealthy people are like Ebenezer Scrooge, selfish penny-pinchers.*
18. *It's a dog-eat-dog world out there, survival of the fittest.*
19. *In climbing the ladder of success, you have to step on others on the way up.*
20. *You have to be in certain professions to make a lot of money.*
21. *Only a few actors (musicians, artists, writers, yada yada) ever make it to the top.*
22. *It's too complicated to organize and track my finances.*
23. *I am not abundant.*
24. *I can't hold/keep money.*
25. *I'm not able to save money.*
26. *I have too much debt and can't save or invest any money.*
27. *I don't have much savings, but I have to contribute to my family.*
28. *I will suddenly run out of money.*
29. *I hate my job, but I'm stuck there.*
30. *I'm worth more than I make.*
31. *I probably won't be given a raise, so I shouldn't bother asking.*
32. *I'll never be able to earn as much money as (.)*
33. *I can't stop spending money.*
34. *My spouse won't support my financial goals.*
35. *Investing is risky; I will lose everything.*

Pick your top 5 limited beliefs from the above that you want to work on and turn them into positive affirmations below that you'll repeat to yourself daily:

1 ....

2 ....

3 ....

4 ....

5 ....

2.3. HOW TO WORK ON LIMITED BELIEFS

Here are the action steps to work on each of your limited beliefs:

1. Bring awareness of the limited belief and fully accept it.
2. Investigate where you embedded that belief and have full understanding with compassion to the person or situation.
3. Repeat daily the positive version of your limited belief for at least 66 days. Use your journal, set a jar with a piece of paper next to it and each time you pass in front of it write down your affirmation to put in the jar, or set an alarm twice a day with your affirmation as a title.
4. Do hypnotherapy with you hardest self-limited beliefs
5. Explore the work of Marissa Pier with her website www.iamenough.com. I Am Enough is the foundation of all limited beliefs.

Abundance Blocks

CHAPTER 3 :

30 minutes to complete

"WHEN YOU ARE GRATEFUL FEAR DISAPPEARS AND ABUNDANCE APPEARS."

~ UNKNOWN

Abundance, a word that is overused by people who don't really understand the core of it. Abundance is a frequency you can tune in to by connecting and becoming that frequency. But how can one do that, you might ask? Abundance is linked to the Root Chakra and the Sacral Chakra. So you need to unblock those vortexes of energy by connecting more and more with them through emotional release, meditation, intention, etc.

For the Root Chakra, which is red and the first vortex of your energetic body that is located at the base of your spine, you need to connect with more earth energy, ground yourself in this physical life, sense your body, and not live in your head, your thoughts. It's easier for women to connect with that chakra because they give birth; therefore, they are connected to the Mother Earth energy.

And, finally, to unblock your Sacral Chakra, which is orange and the 2nd vortex of your energetic body that is located 2 inches below your belly button, you need to connect to your 5 senses, physical pleasure, creativity, your sexual life, and to release trapped emotions, especially any hidden subconscious fears that are stuck in the kidneys.

Feminine energy is linked to the first three Chakras: Root, Sacral, and Solar Plexus, while masculine energy is linked to the three upper Chakras: Throat, Third Eye, and Crown. More about that in the workbook *Become A Multi-Sensory Being* of the *Become Series.*

Here are two small video introductions on the subject:
How to Bring Abundance into Your Life | A New Earth | Oprah Winfrey Network
https://youtu.be/cKc5ZKhtgxA

Attracting Abundance - Bob Proctor
https://youtu.be/dNeLuHmzGVg

3.1. TURN YOUR CHILDHOOD SITUATION INTO ABUNDANCE

1. List your current money patterns (thoughts, beliefs, relationship of money with others, life situation, salary, investment, debt, savings, cash flow, etc.).
Example: Each time I receive a huge amount of money, I tend to spend it fast. I have a lot of debt, zero investment and savings, and I'm living paycheck to paycheck.

2. List your childhood thoughts or experiences around money (parents' conversations, environment, neighborhood, how your friends saw your money situation, school situation, etc.)
Example: I thought I was poor because all my neighborhood friends were richer than me and were making fun of me for it.

3. List all the things you had as a child compared to most poor childhood experiences. (As a child, you compare yourself to your surroundings or what you see on the television, but it's not the full reality. Compare your childhood experiences to the 7+ billion people living on this Earth, 80% are living on less than $10 a day.)

Example: Your parents were bringing you to eat at the restaurant. You received gifts from your uncles and aunties on your birthday.

4. Realize your new childhood mindset around money (rewrite your belief about your childhood situation; you'll most likely see how lucky and grateful you are about your upbringing).

Example: I can't believe I thought I was poor as a child; I was blessed. My parents gave me everything they could. I was so lucky to have my uncle surprise me with little things.

3.2. CLEARING ABUNDANCE BLOCKS

Step by step, you release one after the other. A single block can overshadow or derail your life. Hold an image and the reality of a perfect energy and abundance around you. Then ask what's in the way of that reality. Situations or experiences from the first 7 years of your life are your abundance blocks. Think about your father and mother figure. How did they feel about money? Did you duplicate their energy toward keeping money in abundance?

Each time you release a block, you expand your energy body, your aura. Living more and more in tune with the universe, receiving what you want and seeing synchronicities. When you expand your aura, you live out of higher frequencies from the scale of emotion of David R. Hawkins.

Here are the 24 abundance blocks suggested by Christie Marie Sheldon. You can do her free 1-hour mastermind call "Unblock Your Abundance" on Mindvalley where she goes over the first 7 blocks.

Go over each block one by one and ask your body. Really feel body sensations of contraction or expansion. Most likely in your heart chakra area right in the middle of your chest. For those that are less in touch with their body, most likely men that didn't have much experience from the non-physical world, I suggest using the muscle testing technique to identify your blocks with a "yes or no" question. Just YouTube search "self-muscle testing" or "muscle testing yourself."
Example: Do I have an abundance block of fear of change? Yes or no.

1. **RESISTANCE**

The refusal to accept or comply with something. Avoiding to do something that you know you need to do.

2. **DOUBT AND FEAR**

"Cross Purposes" - Do you ever find yourself worrying about not being good / smart / creative enough?

3. **FEAR OF CHANGE**

Learn to let go of issues you have been avoiding and keeping you disconnected from the source.

4. **MONEY ZAPPING DECISIONS**

All your self-sabotaging money decisions, for example, loading your credit card, not doing your taxes, not having strong personal finance habits, etc.

5. **FEAR OF GROWTH**

You think that if you grow too much maybe the people around you aren't going to like it.

6. **FEAR OF SUCCESS**

Did you grow up surrounded with people that didn't like rich people?

7. **FEAR OF REJECTION**

Are you affected by what other people perceive or see you as? You are scared to ask for the things you want.

8. FEAR OF NUMBERS
Do you know your X amount in your bank right now? X amount of debt? X amount of revenue/salary this year?

9. INDECISION
You have so many opportunities that you don't know which one to take first.

10. FEELING STUCK
Do you have problems keeping constant growth and keeping the energy of change?

11. BE CLEAR ON YOUR VALUES
Identify the values you want to be living and map out the steps toward achieving it.

12. BE CLEAR ON THE FUTURE
Learn the power of getting over things, so you can live easily instead of always standing in the shadow of life's problems.

13. CLUTTER
Your life is cluttered with hundreds of options: messy finance, full email inbox, disorganized room, emotional clutter, etc.

14. FAMILY BLOCKS
Your connection with your core family members; share your love and your life with them.

15. BLAME
Putting things on other people's fault. Or blaming yourself leading to shame.

16. DISCOVER THE ULTIMATE YOU
Do you know the real you, the characteristic of your true self? Unlock all your skills.

17. GENERATE YOUR FUTURE SELF
Manifest your heart's desires.

18. TURNING BLOCKS INTO PROFITS
Own your personal finance habits. Monthly forecasting, budget, accounting. Run yourself as a micro business. Manifest a ton of cash.

19. SELF-SABOTAGE
Whatever you stage in life, you stay authentic, empowering, and real to your heart. Grab hold of your karmic debt.

20. LACK OF SELF-WORTH
Love or lack of it from your parents as a child is affecting how you feel about yourself now. Use source energy to fill your core with unconditional love you may not have received as a child.

21. **FINANCIAL MESS**

The fear of messing up your financials. Reach the perfect balance point between giving and taking.

22. **FINANCIAL ILLUSIONS**

How are you investing? Do you want to become a millionaire overnight? Did you put your money in the right places?

23. **FEAR OF SCARCITY**

Are you generous? Do you feel you have enough?

24. **BLOCKS TO WELCOME ABUNDANCE**

Dig deep inside yourself to find what talents you've been neglecting that could contribute to a higher income and happier days. Contribute to the world with your talents.

Identify all your blocks and explain how you think you got them. If you have doubts identifying them with the suggestion above, go over the section 3.3 below.

3.3. CLEANSING YOUR ABUNDANCE BLOCKS

Cleansing your abundance blocks won't happen instantly. The first step is to bring awareness that we have a specific block, but then we need to move that energy that has been stagnant there for years. This spiritual work might take years, but don't worry the journey is to be enjoyed fully.

1. Muscle testing asks "yes/true" or "no/false" questions. Watch this video: Muscle Test Yourself - 5 Methods! | Whitten Method https://www.youtube.com/watch?v=96Ln1Ay-bTE
2. The Sedona Method requires asking yourself repeatedly: "Would I welcome it?" "Could I let it go?" "Would I let it go?" "When can I let it go?" Try the YouTube meditation call "LET GO Guided Meditation using Sedona Method for HEALING and POSITIVE ENERGY."

3. In meditation, clean and transmute through all dimensions, time, space and reality.
   Do this meditation at 52:35 on Unblock Your Abundance Masterclass with Christie Marie Sheldon

4. To go deeper on cleaning your energetic body, releasing trapped emotions and blocks, I suggest reading and trying one of those experiences: With a bioenergetic doctor, you can do acupuncture with electricity, cuping, magnet, and light therapy. With a Shaman, you can do an Ayahuasca ceremony, Kambo, Rape and Mushroom ceremony.

For more, check out my Medium article call for *Top 22 Life Experiences That Will Make You Meet Your Soul* by Jf Brou.

CHAPTER 4:

30 minutes to complete

Money is Energy

"MONEY IS JUST ENERGY, LEARN TO LOVE THE ENERGY OF MONEY AND YOU WILL ATTRACT MORE OF IT."

What Is Money?

Money is human energy symbolized by papers and coins that allow us to trade it. The love, time, and energy you put into something is really energy, and this energy is the real money. The physical money is just a symbol of the energy we are creating. So, really, money is just like all energy; it's just love. Money energy is giving energy. It's the joy of giving.

This chapter is all about connecting more with that energy and creating a more trustworthy relationship with it, treating money like it was your lover. At the end of this chapter, you'll start seeing money from a different perspective. You'll realize you need to take care of it in a better way and be more gentle, grateful, attentive and delicate with what you think, say, or how you act about it.

4.1. BUILD A STRONG RELATIONSHIP WITH THAT ENERGY

PART 1: IMAGINE MONEY AS AN ANIMAL OR A FRIEND

Imagine money is a being and you have a relationship with it. What does this being look like? What are the circumstances?

Now, whatever that is, change the image into something that makes you feel fun and free around money. For example, Labrador puppies running toward you in the field.

PART 2: A LETTER TO MONEY

1. Write a kind letter to money. Realize that money is an innocent energy that loves to play and help people. Here are the things you should include in your letter:

    A. Tell money what you REALLY think of it. Be totally honest. (Write down the relationship as if money can hear you, like it's a real being.)
    B. Apologize to money for all the negative things you think about it and all the mean things you said about it behind its back.
    C. Apologize as well for the times you've grasped money so hard you hurt it, clinging with talons of desperation that nearly choked it to death.
    D. Also, apologize for times you've been ungrateful to money. Times when it was there for you—as much as it could be—and all you did was complain about how it wasn't doing enough. Appreciate money for all the ways it was there for you and the ways that it helped you.
    E. Tell money that you release it from your anxiety and anger. See it as a creature, an animal that wants to play and love and reproduce.
    F. Offer as much affection as you can. Tell money it's done you no harm (in and of itself) and that you forgive it for all the ways humans misuse it. Love it.
    G. Invite money to come play with you. Try to feel the joy of hosting it in your life, of giving it a place to be safe and warm and dry.
    H. Let it know it can come to you anytime it wants, in any way it wants.

2. Now, pretend you ARE money, and write a letter back to yourself. Become money and write to yourself as money. Tell yourself…

    A. …why money may be avoiding you (write this as "I, money, am avoiding you because…").
    B. …why money wants to come to you ("I, money, want to come to you because…).
    C. …what you could do to invite it in ("I, money, would love it if you would…).
    D. …what you could do to make life more fun for you and your money ("I, money, would love to have fun with you doing…).

3. Take any action you've identified that sounds interesting. Observe the results!

4.2. FIX YOUR MONEY WOUNDS BY PRAISING THAT ENERGY

As we saw in the Ken Honda free Mindvalley masterclass "The Japanese Art of Healing Your Money Wounds".

1. Appreciation/Gratitude of what you have now (80% of the population live on $10 a day).
2. Arigato technique, thank your money in and out. (Each time you pay someone or a bill, thank all the people that made it possible for you to receive this service or product. For example, at the restaurant, mentally thank the waiter, the cook, the restaurant owner, the farmer, the distributor, etc. Also, each time you receive money, thank the person or employer, like this is a never-ending cycle of blessings.)
3. Choose Positive Money Affirmations to live by:
    1. The universe is abundant.
    2. The universe wants ME to prosper.
    3. All prosperity begins with belief.
    4. Money is an abstraction.
    5. Money is energy—and will appear as you really feel about it.
    6. Money has no intelligence of its own.
    7. Money will respond to the instructions I give it.
    8. Money demands attention.

CHAPTER 5 :

30 minutes to complete

"THE BIGGEST ADVENTURE YOU CAN TAKE IS TO LIVE THE LIFE OF YOUR DREAMS."

~ OPRAH WINFREY

Before goal setting, planning, saving, or making investments, we need to identify how much you need to live while being comfortable with a lifestyle that doesn't block you from your growth, but also not so comfortable that you stop chasing your dreams and goals.

5.1. BECOME A BIT MORE MINIMALISTIC

1. Identify 5 things you don't really need that you'll cut right now from your monthly expenses

2. Identify 5 things you'll get rid of in your house

3. Identify 3 actions you'll take to clean your environment. A clean life equals a clean mind.
Example: digital storage, physical storage, wardrobe, house, room, etc.

5.2. HOW MUCH DO YOU NEED FOR EACH OF THOSE EXPENSE CATEGORIES

*Write the amount you wish and are not far from living by.

Here's ratio to keep in mind on your total:

1. Pay myself first. Saving should be around 10%.
2. Rent should be around 30%.
3. Food should be around 30%.
4. Transportation should be around 5%.
5. Recreation should be around 10%.
6. Investment in myself should be around 10%.

HOW MUCH DO YOU NEED FOR EACH OF THOSE EXPENSE CATEGORIES QUIZ	RESULT
1 Pay myself first by saving (see the chapter below)	
2 Rent (including utilities like Internet, phone, electricity, water, cable, etc.)	
3 Food (every month consumption: groceries, restaurants, alcohol, cigarettes, coffee, etc.)	
4 Transportation (taxi, metro, flights, car, gaz, etc.)	
5 Recreation (sports, activities, weekend trips, community, etc.)	
6 Investment in myself (self-care, wardrobe, workshops, books, courses, etc.)	
My total monthly ideal lifestyle	

5.3. 90-DAY FORECAST BUDGET

Yes, plans are not made to be accomplished fully, but they are very useful to help us to be excited and take action. Your goal here is to brainstorm different scenarios, find creative ways to bring more streams of income while always becoming a bit more minimalistic.

Compared to your ideal lifestyle we set above, now, we'll do a short-term realistic forecast to either reach this ideal lifestyle or improve it.

MONTH EXAMPLE

EXAMPLE - MONTH EXPENSES	EXPENSES
1 Pay myself first by saving: (10% of my revenue at each 25th of the month)	$650
2 Rent: (room in a flat sharing)	$800
3 Food: (minimizing restaurant and alcohol)	$500
4 Transportation: (flight, Uber, public transportation)	$350
5 Recreation: (weekend trip, cooking class)	$400
6 Investment in myself: (books, workshops, gym)	$200
Total	$2,550
EXAMPLE - MONTH REVENUE	**REVENUE**
1 Salary: (remote job)	$4,000
2 Freelancing gig: (consultant/coaching)	$1,000
3 Passive Income: (self-published book)	$1,000
4 Investments: (Robinhood)	$500
Total	$6,500
Month Example 1 Profit/Saving:	$3,950

Draft your next 90-day forecast here and then track it on a spreadsheet to see your growth evolution:

MONTH 1

MONTH 1 - EXPENSES	EXPENSES
1 Pay myself first by saving	
2 Rent	
3 Food	
4 Transportation	
5 Recreation	
6 Investment in myself	
Total	
MONTH 1 - REVENUE	**REVENUE**
1 Salary	
2 Freelancing gig	
3 Passive Income	
4 Investments	
Total	
Month 1 Profit/Saving:	

MONTH 2

MONTH 2 - EXPENSES		EXPENSES
1	Pay myself first by saving	
2	Rent	
3	Food	
4	Transportation	
5	Recreation	
6	Investment in myself	
Total		

MONTH 2 - REVENUE		REVENUE
1	Salary	
2	Freelancing gig	
3	Passive Income	
4	Investments	
Total		
Month 2 Profit/Saving:		

MONTH 3

MONTH 3 - EXPENSES	EXPENSES
1 - Pay myself first by saving	
2 - Rent	
3 - Food	
4 - Transportation	
5 - Recreation	
6 - Investment in myself	
Total	
MONTH 3 - REVENUE	**REVENUE**
1 - Salary	
2 - Freelancing gig	
3 - Passive Income	
4 - Investments	
Total	
Month 2 Profit/Saving:	

"A BUDGET IS TELLING YOUR MONEY WHERE TO GO INSTEAD OF WONDERING WHERE IT WENT."

~ DAVE RAMSEY

Making More Money

CHAPTER 6 :

15 minutes to complete

"IF YOU DON'T FIND A WAY TO MAKE MONEY WHILE YOU SLEEP, YOU WILL WORK UNTIL YOU DIE."

- WARREN BUFFETT

There are many ways to start building new sources of income. The goal is to try, take action, fail, and try again. One day, you'll end up with multiple sources of income that might even lead you to be able to take a one-year sabbatical while still growing your net worth. You've probably heard this quote: "The average millionaire has seven sources of income."

Here are 5 types of income you can start researching on and then take action on one or two that fit your current life situation.

6.1. SKILLED REMOTE JOB

It's now easier than ever to work remotely, and real remote company cultures let you manage your own time and even combine different jobs or personal projects. So why not find a 10h/week remote job on top of your full-time job?

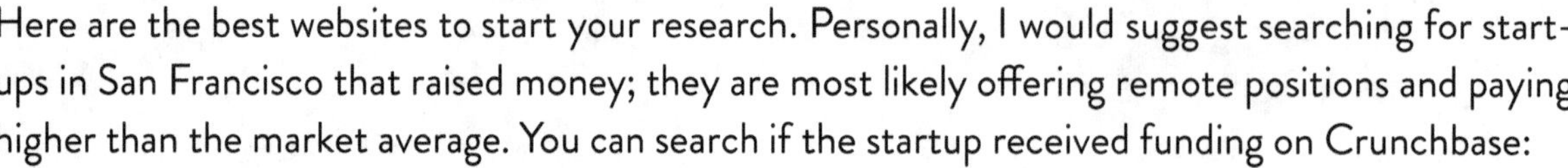

Here are the best websites to start your research. Personally, I would suggest searching for start-ups in San Francisco that raised money; they are most likely offering remote positions and paying higher than the market average. You can search if the startup received funding on Crunchbase:
https://angel.co/jobs
https://workew.com/
https://www.upwork.com/
https://indeed.com/

60 Best Remote Jobs Websites to Find a Great Remote Job (Fast) in 2020:
https://www.ryrob.com/remote-jobs-websites/

Here are the awarded best remote companies, explore their company culture to have a feeling of the flexibilities:
https://automattic.com/about/
https://www.toptal.com/
https://hubstaff.com/about
https://getshogun.com/about

Top 100 Remote Companies Hiring:
https://weworkremotely.com/top-remote-companies

Here's my application process advice to find something quick:

1. Save all potential job offers from 5-10h of research.
2. Select your top 10.
3. Select your top 3 and apply through the job website.
4. Find the LinkedIn of the Manager, HR, CEO, or any person in charge that you think is relevant. Add them on LinkedIn and scrap their email. Here's a list of the best scraping tools: https://www.octoparse.com/blog/best-email-scraping-tools-for-sales-prospecting-in-2019.
5. Send email to your best match lead with your personalized cover letter. Keep your letter short, mention three reasons why you want to work for them and three reasons why you are the best candidate for the job. Make sure to connect their values and company cultures with your values and personality. Here's a cover letter sample below.
6. 2-3 days after, send a second email with a document you have built for the company. Example: Marketing Plan, PPT presentation for a project, a video presentation of yourself, a market research, etc. Also, make sure to send them a message on LinkedIn if they accept you.

Throughout the whole reaching out process, make sure to show high excitement, creativity, and deep research on the company and managers.

Here's my cover letter example:

Dear FIRST NAME,

I'm JF (Jean-Francois), an entrepreneur with 9 years of experience and would love to join your team.

I've launched a few failed businesses like the Rep Your Flag Festival, but my biggest project is InterStude. A bus tour operator based in Canada working on a niche market.

My strength is producing product-market fit and marketing campaigns with the help of visual specialists like Graphic Designer, Video Editor, Cameraman, and Content Writer while using all kinds of organic growth hacking techniques to sell those B2C products/services. I LOVE MARKETING, LIFE EXPERIENCES, and SELF-DEVELOPMENT, as you can see in my portfolio of projects here: http://jfbrou.com/

I believe with my skills and experiences, as the Marketing Manager of your company, I can:

- Produce creative marketing content for multiple channels growing our social proof and client base (example in my portfolio from video trailers, to articles, books, live events, and travel experiences).

- Grow and strengthen the community with check-in, challenges, content, masterminds, accountable buddies, book club, and many more ideas (experiences running communities on Slack, FB groups, Discord, live with weekly cultural events).

- Create unique lead generators connected with a high conversion funnel while always updating and improving our database of leads (experiences mastering Clickfunnel and Leadpages while creating top beautiful e-books).

Why I want to work for your COMPANY:

- To connect and learn from the organization's incredible network and members.

- To join the small passionate team supporting each other and wanting to grow together.

- To impact fellow Canadian entrepreneurs and startups with strong resources.

Can't wait to have news from you, FIRST NAME :)

BOOKS:

The Year Without Pants: WordPress.com and the Future of Work by Scott Berkun
Remote: Office Not Required by David Heinemeier Hansson and Jason Fried

6.2. GIGS

Now, on the Internet, there are all kinds of non-skilled gigs that even a high school student could do. Why not create a small weekly gig that will allow you to bounce back if any life crises happen? Also, it will allow you to be a more versatile team player in an organization.

AI verification: Appen.com
Customer Interviews: Respondent.com, Userinterviews.com
Online Surveys: Surveyjunkie.com, Swagbucks.com
Sharing Economy: TaskRabbit, Uber, Bird, Instacart
Tutoring: VIPkid, SuperProf
Volunteering Travel Expenses Covered: Woofing, Workaway
Writing: Blog or Copywriting (search on YouTube top blog websites to write for), Contena
Sitting: Rover.com (dog sitting), trustedhousesitters.com (house sitting), aupair.com (baby-sitting)
Small Business Social Media Management: Check out the Tai Lopez course SMMA 3.0 at smmaofficial.com

RESOURCES:
https://www.sidehustlenation.com/ideas/
https://millo.co/remote-writing-jobs
https://www.sidehustlenation.com/consumer-research-companies-online-focus-groups/

BOOK:
The Gig Economy: The Complete Guide to Getting Better Work, Taking More Time Off, and Financing the Life You Want by Diane Mulcahy

6.3. PASSIVE INCOMES

If you have skills or experiences to share, you could monetize them, build a service that would eventually bring you a steady stream of income.

Online Course: Udemy, Skillshare, Teachable
Self-Publishing Books: CreateSpace, Ingramspark
E-Commerce: Dropshipping, T-shirt print demand, Etsy
Room Rental: Airbnb, Uniplace
Affiliate: ClickBank, Amazon, AdSense
Photo/Video Licensing: iStock, 500px, Shutterstock

To get started, take a course online that will teach you the step-by-step process of the passive income that you want to tackle first. Access all the top courses online here for a 100$ membership:
https://www.getwsodo.com/spreadsheet/

BOOKS:

The $100 Startup: Reinvent the Way You Make a Living, Do What You Love, and Create a New Future by Chris Guillebeau
Click Millionaires: Work Less, Live More with an Internet Business You Love by Scott Fox
The 4-Hour Workweek: Escape 9-5, Live Anywhere, and Join the New Rich by Timothy Ferriss
Passive Income, Aggressive Retirement: The Secret to Freedom, Flexibility, and Financial Independence (& how to get started!) by Rachel Richards

6.4. SIDE HUSTLES

A side hustle is a small business you can start part time at night with very little investment. Chris Guillebeau is the go-to resource to dig deep into the mindset and hear people's stories. Get his books and listen to his podcast and maybe some creative idea will come to you.

RESOURCES:

https://sidehustleschool.com/
https://chrisguillebeau.com/100-days-side-hustle-school/

6.5. SMALL INVESTMENTS

Once you are making enough money to cover your ideal comfortable lifestyle, it's time to build more wealth and resources with small investments that allow you to hide money from yourself.

Peer to Peer Lending: LendingClub, LengindLoop
Real Estate: Fundrise, RealtyMogul, REIG Investing
Equities: Robinhood, Stash, EquityBee, Fidelity
Flipping Website: EmpireFlippers, Flippa
Mobile App: BuildFire

RESOURCES:

https://medium.com/@jfbrou/pay-yourself-first-investment-of-1k-5k-15k-bringing-you-passive-income-511dabf7f53a

6.6. PLAN AND TAKE ACTIONS

Based on your research and resources above, answer the following:

1. List your skills

2. List your resources

3. Why do you want to make more money?

4. What is your next monthly income goal to reach that and why?

5. Which side hustle type fits you best?

6. List your 3 best money stream opportunities

7. Make a 5-step action plan to act on in 14 days

8. Share your plan to your community, friend, or family member to be accountable

6.7. RECEIVING A RAISE AS AN EMPLOYEE

Here are 3 amazing resources to understand the basics and depth of salary negotiation in all kinds of situations:
https://www.themuse.com/advice/how-to-negotiate-salary-37-tips-you-need-to-know
https://www.glassdoor.com/blog/guide/how-to-negotiate-your-salary/
https://www.indeed.com/career-advice/pay-salary/how-to-negotiate-salary

BOOK:
Never Split the Difference: Negotiating as if Your Life Depended on It by Chriss Voss

Based on your research and resources above, answer the following:

1. What is your exact yearly and hourly salary number value based on your skills, job position, and country you want to work in? Again, here are some factors that can influence your value: geographic location, years of industry experience, years of leadership experience, education level, career level, skills, licenses, and certifications.

2. What are the perks, advantages, and/or little add-ons you would like to add into your negotiation?

3. List 3 salary negotiation techniques you would like to practice before making your big move?

4. Write down your offer in a letter you could potentially send via email or just keep as a rehearsal for your big day 1-on-1 negotiation

CHAPTER 7 :

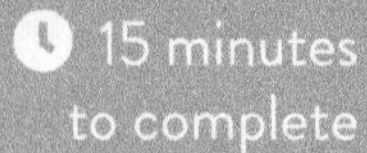

15 minutes to complete

Pay Your Debt

"PAY OFF YOUR DEBT FIRST.
FREEDOM FROM DEBT IS WORTH MORE
THAN ANY AMOUNT OF MONEY YOU CAN EARN."

~ MARK CUBAN

When you have a bad-debt-to-income ratio you just become a slave of the society. Your energy body aura is contracted on itself. You live out of fears, anxiety, worries, scarcity, instability, depression, and low self-esteem, which is a very hard loop to get out of. You are literally living out of a blocked Root chakra, the 1st chakra, which is a red color at the base of your pelvic floor that is linked to stability and grounding to the Earth.

7.1. DEBT REPAYMENT STRATEGY

https://www.nerdwallet.com/blog/pay-off-debt/
https://www.nerdwallet.com/blog/credit-card-debt/

Here are some common strategies to boost your payoff speed:
DEBT SNOWBALL: You focus on paying off your smallest debt first (while paying minimums on the others), then roll the amount you had been paying on it into payments on the next largest debt.

DEBT AVALANCHE: You pay off your debt with the highest interest rate first (while paying minimums on the others), then the next highest rate, and so on. It may save you time and money over the course of your debt payoff.

DEBT CONSOLIDATION: Combine multiple old debts into a single new one, ideally at a lower interest rate, making payments more manageable or the payoff period shorter. There are a few ways to consolidate debt, including balance transfer cards and personal loans.

DEBT MANAGEMENT PLAN: If you're facing a mountain of credit card debt and not making much progress, a nonprofit credit counseling agency can set up a debt management plan to cut your interest rate and put you on a repayment plan.

How much is your total debt: ....

Which strategy will you choose: ....

What is the first action you'll take: ....

7.2. GROW YOUR CREDIT SCORE

1. What is your credit score now? ....
2. What is your credit score goal in 12 months? ....
3. What are the 3 action steps you'll take to reach your credit score goal?

....

....

....

CHAPTER 8 :

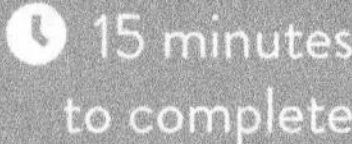

15 minutes to complete

Pay Yourself First

"DO NOT SAVE WHAT IS LEFT AFTER SPENDING BUT SPEND WHAT IS LEFT AFTER SAVING."

~ - WARREN BUFFET

No matter your income, the key to riches is the "Pay Yourself First" principle from the bestselling book *The Richest Man in Babylon* by George Samuel Clason and also developed in the most recent book *Profit First* by Mike Michalowicz.

The principle states that you should pay yourself as soon as your income comes into your bank account. Before paying any expenses and bills, you transfer yourself 10–20% into a frozen separate account only someone you trust has access to. You need to hide money from yourself. Then the goal is to grow this account into a planned number so you'll be able to use that money for a small investment that will bring you monthly or quarterly passive income. We are looking to grow liquidity here, not a long-term investment.

To start building the habit, I highly suggest making a minimum investment of $1,000 every 2 months. If you wait more than 2 months to empty your investment account to pay your investment, you are most likely going to have to use that money to pay for unexpected things happening in your life or business. This principle is taking into account human psychological behavior of always spending what's available and always finding creative ways to pay last-minute bills.

8.1. PLAN YOUR FIRST PAY-YOURSELF-FIRST INVESTMENT

		RESULT
1	Choose a meaningful date number you'll put money aside every month (example, the 23rd, because it's my anniversary date):	
2	How much you'll put aside every month:	
3	Where you'll hide this money from yourself (block blank account, family member):	
4	How the transfer will be made (make it automatic if you can):	
5	How much you'll save in your first 2-3 months to then invest it:	
6	Where you'll invest that first pay-yourself-first investment:	
7	How much monthly return your first investment will make you and after how many months after the investment:	
8	What are the 2-3 other investment ideas you think you'll do in the next 12 months:	
9	Where could you receive more knowledge about small investment opportunities (blog site, entrepreneur friend, mastermind group, etc.):	

INVESTMENT IDEAS:

1. Investments of $1k to $3k
2. Self-publish a book on Amazon
3. Passive real estate funds like Fundrise
4. Create an online course on Udemy
5. Peer to peer lending like Lending Club
6. Invest in your favorite companies with Robinhood
7. Start a side hustle learning from Chris Guillebeault

INVESTMENTS OF $3K TO $7K

1. Sublet an Airbnb 3–5-room apartments
2. Start an online business with Shopify
3. Buy a running online business with Empire Flippers

INVESTMENTS OF $7K TO $15K

1. Create a mobile app

INVESTMENTS OF $15K AND MORE

1. Invest in real estate
2. Be an Angel Investor in a startup

For more investment ideas, check out these resources:
https://medium.com/@jfbrou/pay-yourself-first-investment-of-1k-5k-15k-bringing-you-passive-income-511dabf7f53a
https://www.ruleoneinvesting.com/blog/investing-news-and-tips/small-investment-ideas-for-investing-500/
https://www.goodfinancialcents.com/how-to-invest-small-amounts-of-money/
https://moneycheck.com/investment-ideas-for-millennials/
https://millennialmoney.com/how-to-start-investing-with-little-money/

8.2. SAVE MONEY IN A SAFE HAVEN

Personally, I wouldn't save money in a savings bank account. Firstly, because the interest rate is lower than the inflation rate, so you're losing money over time. Secondly, because it's too easy to access this money in terms of needs, you want to hide it from yourself. It's human psychology that we'll see in a later chapter. Thirdly, 62% of millennials hate banks.

The right way to save money is different from the economic situations, so for us now in 2020 with the Coronavirus crisis your safe heaven is Gold, Silver, and Bitcoin, as suggested many times by Robert Kiyosaki in his latest podcast.

Most people save their money on the stock market with the most popular stocks or index funds while also saving in their 401K (retirement account). But as mentioned by Robert there are rumors that there's no more money in the pension funds and there are too many old people right now in retirement. Also, the stock market in an economic crisis like we are living now is too volatile to hold your money there.

All Baby Boomers are retiring right now and spending less money on retirement, records governments debts worldwide, central banks are trying to stimulate economies by printing trillions of dollars and giving free monthly allowances to millions of people, etc. There's so much going on right now that we are experiencing a massive financial crisis and even total crash of the Fiat currencies system (Fiat money is a government-issued currency that isn't backed by a commodity such as gold).

So think of Bitcoin as an option in a future financial system.

Here are resources for your safe haven:

GOLD:

Buy physical gold bars in your country and hide it in a safe place. Gold just reached its all-time high since 2011 of $1,920.30 and experts predict that it will go up to $3000.

Here's a great article to get you started: *How Do You Purchase Physical Gold Bars?* on Investopedia.com

SILVER:

You could also buy gold and silver and hold it on an exchange, but make sure that it's a solid company that will survive a deep financial crisis. The country of Singapore is known to be a safe haven in terms of the financial system that should survive a world crisis. So I would suggest holding Silver in Singapore via www.silverbullion.com.sg

BITCOIN:

With more and more institutions integrating the possibilities of accepting Bitcoins, the masses will slowly accept that it's here to stay, so demand will go higher. PayPal is partnering with Paxful to work on offering their 325 million users an option to buy cryptocurrency very soon. You can rest assured that from PayPal's move, Visa and MasterCard will follow. Bitcoin just hit an all-time high this year and finally bust the significant bar of $10,000.

BITCOIN RESOURCES:

Exchanges:

3. Bitstamp
4. Coinbase
5. Binance

News:

1. Coindesk.com
2. Cointelegraph.com
3. Rich Dad YouTube Channel

Banks:

1. Crypto.com
2. BlockFy.com

CHAPTER 9 :

> "THE ONLY THING THAT HURTS MORE THAN PAYING INCOME TAX IS NOT HAVING TO PAY AN INCOME TAX."
>
> ~ THOMAS DEWAR

As an entrepreneur or freelancer, it is a very hard feeling to end up having to pay the government at the end of the year after doing your income taxes. The best way to not have a heart attack at the end of the year and having to pay money you don't have any more is to prepare yourself and know the game fully. There are many tax credits your country offers you and there're many loopholes you can use while investing your money. It is your responsibility to find the resources and contacts depending on your life situation.

9.1. TAXES CREDIT TIPS

https://www.nerdwallet.com/blog/taxes/tax-deductions-tax-breaks/
https://www.nerdwallet.com/blog/taxes/tips-save-taxes/

Based on your research and resources above, answer the following:

1. Which tax credits do you have access to in your country in your current situation?

....

....

....

2. How much taxes will you pay this year without the credits?

3. How much taxes will you pay this year with the credits?

9.2. OFFSHORE OPTIONS

The best resources I encountered on the subject is Nomad Capitalist with these in-depth YouTube videos and free articles: https://nomadcapitalist.com/

There's also a book to deepen your understanding: *Nomad Capitalist: How to Reclaim Your Freedom with Offshore Bank Accounts, Dual Citizenship, Foreign Companies, and Overseas Investments* https://www.amazon.com/Nomad-Capitalist-Citizenship-Companies-Investments-ebook/dp/B07C2QK2ML

Personally, my 2 easiest offshore options to start your journey are:
https://e-resident.gov.ee/welcome/
https://stripe.com/atlas

Based on your research and resources above, answer the following:

1. Which offshore country will you open an account in and why this one?

CHAPTER 10 :

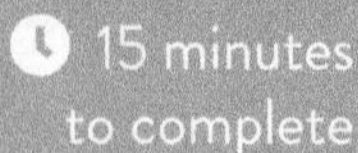

15 minutes to complete

Retirement Dreams

"THE QUESTION ISN'T AT WHAT AGE I WANT TO RETIRE, IT'S AT WHAT INCOME."

~ GEORGE FOREMAN

If you are in your 20s or early 30s, you are probably like me and never want to think about your retirement and your old days. Don't worry, it's normal. But at the same time if your only retirement plan is to become rich and/or never stop working, I think you need to reach a point of maturity and should start having a plan B. Because, yes, bad luck happens and you might not be as healthy as you wish in your old days. The goal here is not to set a precise retirement plan because, yes, who knows what you'll do in 10 years, but at least start thinking about it and bring awareness to the fact that you should slowly start having a better idea about retirement.

10.1.RETIREMENT VISION

		RESULT
1	At what age do you wish to stop working:	
2	What would you like to do in your retirement? List any passion project like "I would like to run my own small family on the coast of Italy;" "I want to travel the world on a cruise;" "I want to write a novel;" "I want to help young children in a third world country;" etc.:	
3	For how many years do you think you'll be in retirement:	
4	From what you want to do of your retirement, what would be your monthly lifestyle expenses:	
5	How much is this lifestyle per year:	
6	How much is this for your entire retirement:	

10.2. RETIREMENT PLAN

		RESULT
1	Split down into income categories your yearly retirement lifestyle expenses noted above.	
	How much would come yearly from each of those categories:	
	Savings:	
	Government retirement funds:	
	Passive Incomes:	
	Investments:	
	Other:	
2	What are the potential problems you might face in your plans?	

Financial Habits

CHAPTER 11:

60 minutes to complete

"IT IS NOT YOUR SALARY THAT MAKES YOU RICH; IT'S YOUR SPENDING HABITS."

~ CHARLES A. JAFFE

11.1. BAD FINANCIAL HABITS

Underline all your bad financial habits below that you need to work on in the next few months:

1. Overspending with credit
2. Neglecting a monthly budget
3. Impulse buying
4. Overspending on monthly expenses
5. Missing monthly credit card payments
6. Neglecting long-term planning
7. No contingency planning
8. Redundant spending
9. Not taking advantage of better pricing
10. Neglecting product maintenance

Choose 3 habits you'll focus on and state how you'll take action on removing them.

11.2. GOOD FINANCIAL HABITS

Underline your good financial habits below that you do right now in your life.

1. Live within your means
2. Explore your money patterns, limited beliefs, and abundance blocks
3. Become more of a minimalist, reduce your lifestyle
4. Pay yourself first
5. Do your financial forecast every trimester
6. Pay your debts and taxes
7. Be grateful for your flow of money, each time you pay and receive
8. Only borrow to use it as leverage to make more money
9. Read, watch, and learn about personal finance education every month
10. Track your spending
11. Build new streams of income
12. Learn to say no to yourself or friends pushing you to spend
13. Start a retirement plan
14. Refresh your emergency fund
15. Give to others
16. Improve your relationship with the energy of money
17. Visualize financial freedom
18. Set up your savings automatic transfer
19. Share your money goal with a friend
20. Set up automatic bill payments
21. Work on improving your credit score
22. Maintain an emergency fund

Choose 3 new good financial habits that you want to work on right now:

1 ....

2 ....

3 ....

11.3.HOW TO BUILD HABITS

We build habits by setting the smallest daily goal, as stated by the Kaizen principle[1] that you will build for 66 days so it becomes a part of you, for example, brushing your teeth (you'll feel bad if you don't brush your teeth one morning). It is also suggested to find a trigger to do the habit, like setting an alarm for it. Then you should find a tiny reward. In the case of brushing your teeth, it's having a clean sensation of freshness in your mouth. The book *The One Thing* by Gary Keller states that you can't chase two rabbits at the same time or else you won't catch either of them. Therefore, we should build one habit at a time, which gives us the opportunity to build 5 life-changing habits per year.

In the next chapter, we'll analyze in depth which core habits we should build to change our financial life.

1 According to the Kaizen philosophy, a series of small improvements made continuously over a long period of time can result in drastic improvement in business processes. https://www.brighthubpm.com/project-planning/100172-explaining-the-kaizen-principle/

CHAPTER 12 :

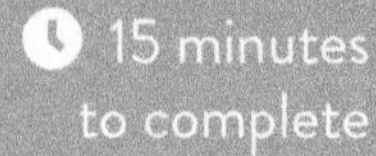

15 minutes to complete

"FAILING TO PLAN IS PLANNING TO FAIL."

~ ALAN LAKEIN

Finance is one of your wheels of life dimensions, as we saw in the workbook *Become Your Best Version*. It is very important to keep the wheel balanced, otherwise you won't roll properly toward your growth and future. Ask yourself where you would like to be someday with this finance dimension and bring this long-term goal to a daily habit.

12.1.GOAL SETTINGS TO THE NOW!

SOMEDAY GOAL

What is the ONE THING I want to do/be/accomplish someday with my finance dimension?

Ex: Someday, I will be financially free of debt and working for money.

FIVE-YEAR GOAL

What is the ONE THING I need to do in five years to accomplish my someday goal?

Ex: To accomplish my someday goal, I need in 5 years to have 3 streams of passive income covering my modest lifestyle expenses.

ONE-YEAR GOAL

What is the ONE THING I need to do in one year to accomplish my five-year goal?

Ex: To accomplish my 5-year goal, I need, in 1 year, to find a mentor and coach that can help me achieve the financial goals and lifestyle I am looking for.

ONE-MONTH GOAL

What is the ONE THING I need to do in one month to accomplish my one-year goal?

Ex: To accomplish my 1-year goal, I need, in 1 month, to finish this "Become Financially Free" workbook and take action on the new knowledge.

ONE-WEEK GOAL

What is the ONE THING I need to do in one week to accomplish my one month goal?

Ex: To accomplish my 1-month goal, I need, in 1 week to start a weekly check-in form. I'll fill it out every Sunday to follow up on my financial habits and actions.

TODAY'S GOAL *(A daily Kaizen principle habit you'll keep consistent on for the next 66 days till it's embedded into a lifestyle).*

What is the ONE THING I need to do today to accomplish my one week goal?

Ex: To accomplish my 1-week and someday goal, I need to take action today on working 5 minutes daily on all facets of my financial life, tracking, reporting, analyzing, and improving till I reach financial freedom.

NOW GOAL *(An accountability action you need to take now. Ex: post on social media your long-term plan or tell a family member).*
What is the ONE THING I need to do now to accomplish my goal today?
Ex: To accomplish my today and someday goal, I will share my goals to my friends and family for full accountability.

....

Find the lead domino and whack away at it until it falls. The lead domino is the habit that will make many others fall. For example, running daily early in the morning will lead you to stop going out to drink, smoke, and eat fast food. For the finance dimension, the lead domino habit is autodidact financial education on a daily basis. The lead domino needs to be the smallest daily habit, as stated by the Kaizen principle[1], that you will build for 66 days so it becomes implemented into you as a lifestyle.

What is the minimum daily goal habit that will whack away other habits and improve this dimension you need to fix and might also improve 2 other wellness life dimensions?

I am committing to ....(specific habit)

for ....(minimum goal of kaizen principle).

What will trigger me to start this habit is

....

(cue: LOCATION, TIME, EMOTIONAL STATE, ACTIONS OF OTHER PEOPLE, IMMEDIATELY PRECEDING LAST ACTIONS, etc.)

and my reward after finishing is ....(reward) that I slowly start craving this habit daily. I'm committing 66 days in a row to this habit to make it a lifestyle.

---

[1] According to the Kaizen philosophy, a series of small improvements made continuously over a long period of time can result in drastic improvement in business processes. https://www.brighthubpm.com/project-planning/100172-explaining-the-kaizen-principle/

Visualize Financial Freedom

CHAPTER 13 :

60 minutes to complete

"WHEN A WEALTHY PERSON REACHES THEIR GOAL, IT IS EXACTLY WHAT THEY EXPECTED, PRECISELY BECAUSE, THROUGH VISUALIZATION THEY'VE BEEN THERE."

~ BOB PROCTOR

The universe serves you with everything you command and is connected through the frequencies you emanate. Your goal is, through a deep meditative state, to bring yourself there present in the wished vision moment. You open wide your Third Eye chakra, looking up through your eyelids fixing the point right in the middle of your forehead and see yourself living every piece of this moment.

Connect with your 5 senses, what you see, smell, touch, hear, and taste. Once you have a clear movie vision happening in your 3rd eye, it's time to connect it with an open heart chakra. Put all your attention right in the middle of your chess; you should feel an expansion and even see some taint of green over your closed eyelids. Once your heart chakra is expanded, feel every sensation link to your vision. Example: You might feel love, gratitude, peace, bliss, ecstasy, etc. All the higher emotions.

To help your connection with the third eye and the heart chakra, you can use their respective frequencies, mudras, or even quartz. Just Google it.

13.1. WRITTEN VERSION IN THE PRESENT TENSE

30 minutes to complete

A 3-year vision written in the present tense mentioning your ideal lifestyle, financial habits, and forecast. Envision the living moments where you create wealth. What do you do, see, touch, hear, or smell? How do you spend your money? What do you do with all that wealth?

Here's a small example to help you break the white page:

In 2023, my financial life will be abundant. I am currently having no money problems, worries, debt. Money is flowing freely and regularly towards me. My relationship with my money is very strong, I'm thanking people when I pay or receive money, blessing the flow of money. I currently have 3 passive incomes, which are helping me cover all the costs of my current lifestyle. I'll start to give more and more of my time and money to the organization and people I truly care about.

To be continued...

In 20........ (year), my financial life is

13.2. MAKE A FINANCIAL VISION BOARD

30 minutes to complete

This is why cavemen drew their dinners on the rocks before hunting. Use canva.com to translate your vision visually with photos, quotes, statements, models, drawing, colors, etc. Carry this visualization tool with you every day in your phone or laptop background and hang it in a place you see it daily. Do a draft here with 6 core photos summarizing your financial vision.

Here are examples of images you can gather in your vision board collage: you giving meals to children in poor situations, a new professional camera (or whatever tool you need for your hobby), a plane flying over an exotic destination, holding 1 Bitcoin, a beautiful beach house, a screenshot of your Revolut bank account with 5000$ in it, piles of 2-3 gold bars, a vault of silver coins, etc.

Then the plan is to do a manifestation meditation with it 1-2 times a week.

Here are the mediation steps:

1. Observe and analyze your vision board.
2. Sit on the floor with your spine straight to keep your chakras open.
3. Put your hands on your lap, palm facing up, tip of thumb finger (fire element). connecting the tip of the index finger (air element). With this mudra, called Gyan Mudra, we are commanding the universe connecting with our third eye.
4. Close your eyes, keep the tip of your tongue on the roof of your mouth to keep your jaw relaxed, and connect the flow of energy in your body.
5. Start the meditation connecting with your third eye looking up toward the middle of your forehead. Project images of you living your vision: What are you doing with your money? How's your relationship with money? How are you helping people's financial problems? Watch it like a movie is happening on your forehead. You feel a tinglish sensation right in the middle of your forehead.
6. Once you have a clear vision happening, bring it down to your heart chakra in the middle of your chest. Feel any positive emotions and sensation happening: bliss, love, joy, peace, etc. Feel it deeply like it's already yours; there's no doubt the universe will make it happen for you.
7. Don't move an inch throughout the whole 10-15-minute meditation and you should feel your aura, energetic body, expand toward higher frequency.

Here's a YouTube manifestation:
10-Minute Manifestation Meditation (Powerful Visualisation)
https://www.youtube.com/watch?v=NVPrxcR_RZI&

13.3. 3-YEAR VISION OF MONEY HELL

30 minutes to complete

Write an opposite 3-year vision of HELL of how your life will be if you don't act on solving your financial problems, realizing your financial dreams, and building those financial habits.

CHAPTER 14 : Gratitude

15 minutes to complete

"I MANIFEST ABUNDANCE WITH GRATITUDE FOR ALL I ALREADY HAVE."

~ UNKNOWN

Like everything else in your life, gratitude is really the foundation; it's the frequency that will allow you to stay at peace while flowing elegantly forward. I really like the Arigato technique of Ken Honda; it makes so much sense. Each time you pay someone or a bill, thank all the people that made it possible for you to receive this service or product. For example, at the restaurant, mentally thank the waiter, the cook, the restaurant owner, the farmer, the distributor, etc. Also, each time you receive money, thank the person or employer, like this is a never-ending cycle of blessings.

14.1. GRATITUDE ENUMERATION

10 minutes to complete

We need a vision to grow, but we need to be grounded, grateful, and humble of what we have been through, and of what we have now. Our goal is to live in the now at every situation, moment, second while blocking time for planning, visualizing and asking the universe. Act like you'll die tomorrow; grow like you'll live 100 years. Write a 5-10-line gratitude statement of your financial situation, of what you have now, how blessed you are compared to 80% of the population living on less than $10 a day.

Example: *How lucky I am to have food on the table and a roof over my head. How lucky I am to have my parents alive supporting my dreams. How lucky I am to have strong friendships with people I can count on in case of problems.*

14.2. "I AM" FINANCIAL AFFIRMATION STATEMENTS

5 minutes to complete

Strengthen yourself by talking to yourself with "I AM" affirmations every day.
Example:

1. *I am abundant.*
2. *I am financially free.*
3. *I am rich.*
4. *I am wealthy.*
5. *I am a minimalist.*
6. *I am a saver.*
7. *I am emotionally intelligent financially.*

I AM ....

I AM ....

I AM ....

I AM ....

I AM ....

I AM ....

I AM ....

I AM ....

I AM ....

14.3. MEDITATION ON ATTRACTING MONEY

1. 5 Ways to INSTANTLY Align with the Energy of Money & Abundance | Powerful Law of Attraction Secrets
   https://www.youtube.com/watch?v=bHs7dgLXWIc&

2. Eliminating Your Money Blocks to Allow More Financial Abundance
   https://www.youtube.com/watch?v=6UgexRahXdA&

3. Attract HUGE Amounts of Money Instantly!! Money Affirmations Meditation | Extremely Powerful!!
   https://www.youtube.com/watch?v=5WpzIUD9rEY

4. Bob Proctor - Money Affirmations (LISTEN TO THIS EVERY DAY!)
   https://www.youtube.com/watch?v=KkFtcQUHO9w

5. Reiki Healing to Clear Financial Blocks
   https://www.youtube.com/watch?v=7Il1fh4eqn8

6. How to Clear Money Blocks FAST! Use THIS to Attract Money Abundance & Wealth (Law of Attraction)
   https://www.youtube.com/watch?v=pqeXGp7E3Zs

7. Citrine Simple 40 Day Money Ritual
   https://www.youtube.com/watch?v=znpHmSvow

14.4. BONUS: 30 DAYS #FINANCIALLYFREE CHALLENGE

Accomplish these 5 steps to get a chance to get one of the private 30-minutecoaching sessions with me.

- Follow me on Facebook @jbrouentrepreneur and Instagram @jfbrou
- Post a photo or video proof of each of the steps on Instagram, Facebook, or YouTube with the hashtag of the steps and #financiallyfree

Steps:

1. Finish this workbook and give an online review on Amazon or Goodreads. #becomefinanciallyfreeworkbook #financiallyfree
2. Have a loved one start the workbook. #lifeisbettertogether #financiallyfree
3. Take a creative financial abundance photo with the workbook. #iamabundant #financiallyfree
4. Print and post in your home your financial abundance photo as a reminder and visualization. #iattractabundance #financiallyfree
5. Give your money, time, and resources to someone or something that counts for you.

I'll randomly choose 5 abundant self-explorers on the 1st of each month and announce them on my Facebook page @jbrouentrepreneur.

Conclusion

"MONEY IS LIFE ENERGY THAT WE EXCHANGE AND USE AS A RESULT OF THE SERVICE WE PROVIDE TO THE UNIVERSE."

~ DEEPAK CHOPRA

Wow, you have done it!!!

Now, it's time to jump and fall as many times as possible toward being financially free; it's the only way. Be consistent every day, never ever give up, be hopeful, keep the excitement flowing, and always be grateful for the journey. Happiness won't happen when you'll succeed, but it's found inside you at every micro moment. Live in total gratitude and you'll be more and more grounded, balancing your root chakra and connecting with the frequency of abundance.

Thank you so much for doing this workbook, it means everything to me. I've put all my love and experiences here to hopefully make an impact. My intention was to give what I wish I had received during my education. Each time I hear someone doing my workbook, it warms my heart chakra with bliss. Don't be shy to reach out on Facebook or Instagram @jfbrou

I hope you can share this workbook with your friends and family so that you can all push each other to the next level. Please don't forget to write a review on Amazon; your support means everything.

Remember, all the answers are inside you. Meditate and connect with the universe.

Jf Brou

Appendix 1

TOP FINANCIAL SERVICES

TOP DIGITAL BANKS

https://www.revolut.com/
https://transferwise.com/gb/borderless/card
https://monese.com/
https://n26.com/en-us

TOP OFFSHORE SERVICES

https://nomadcapitalist.com/
https://e-resident.gov.ee/welcome/
https://stripe.com/atlas

TOP ACCOUNTING TOOLS

For Freelancers: Option 1 Waveapps, Option 2 Freshbooks
For Business: Option 1 Xero, Option 2 QuickBooks
For Personal Finance: Mint

Appendix 2

TOP CONTENT TO READ, WATCH OR LISTEN TO

TOP BOOKS TO READ

Rich Dad, Poor Dad by Robert by Robert T. Kiyosaki
What the Rich Teach Their Kids About Money That the Poor and Middle Class Do Not!
Amazon - Video Summary - Best Article - TedTalk

Richest man in Babylon by George S. Clason
"Our acts can be no wiser than our thoughts."
Amazon - Video Summary - Best Article

The Intelligent Investor by Benjamin Graham
The Definitive Book on Value Investing. A Book of Practical Counsel
Amazon - Video Summary - Best Article

Think and Grow Rich by Napoleon Hill
The Landmark Bestseller Now Revised and Updated for the 21st Century
Amazon - Video Summary - Best Article

The 4-Hour Workweek by Tim Ferriss
Escape 9-5, Live Anywhere, and Join the New Rich
Amazon - Video Summary - Best Article

Financial Freedom by Grand Sabatier
A Proven Path to All the Money You Will Ever Need
Amazon - Video Summary - Best Article

I Will Teach You to Be Rich by Ramit Sethi
"There is a limit to how much you can cut but there is no limit to how much you can earn."
Amazon - Video Summary - Best Article

The Total Money Makeover by Dave Ramsey
A Proven Plan for Financial Fitness
Amazon - Video Summary - Best Article

Profit First by Mike Michalowicz
Transform Your Business from a Cash-Eating Monster to a Money-Making Machine
Amazon - Video Summary - Best Article - TedTalk

TOP ARTICLES TO READ

The Rich Dad Company Statement
https://www.richdad.com/MediaLibrary/RichDad/pdfs/I-Am-The-Rich-Dad-Company.pdf

Rich Dad Balance Sheet
https://www.richdad.com/MediaLibrary/RichDad/pdfs/Balance-Sheet_icon-page.pdf

NomadCapitalist // All the offshore secrets
https://nomadcapitalist.com/

Apply for Your Estonia E-Residency
https://e-resident.gov.ee/welcome/

3 Steps to Get Your Cash "Mask" and Postpone All Your Bills Until Next Year
https://medium.com/@josemunozlife/3-steps-to-get-your-cash-mask-and-postpone-all-your-bills-until-next-year-803f9aae957d

20 Money Blocks That Are Keeping You Broke (and How to Overcome Them
https://www.goodbyetobroke.com/money-blocks/

10 Ways To Clear Your Money Blocks Today
https://www.houseofbrazen.com/2018/07/10-ways-to-clear-your-money-blocks.html

24 Abundance Blocks Holding You Back
https://www.forwardstepsblog.com/2012/03/abundance-blocks/

Which Are the Best Root Chakra Stones and Crystals?
https://angelgrotto.com/crystals-stones/root-chakra/

The Top 16 Must-Read Books on Abundance That Can Help You Attract Greater Wealth into Your Life
https://www.bravethinkinginstitute.com/blog/life-transformation/books-on-abundance-wealth

TOP VIDEOS TO WATCH

The Profit First Concept TEDx Talk
https://www.youtube.com/watch?v=-8O2Rw8moHs

Total Money Makeover by Dave Ramsey
https://www.youtube.com/watch?v=ouRWLK4W66c

What Is An Offshore Bank Account?
https://www.youtube.com/watch?v=c__01NUWqCw

ESTONIAN E-RESIDENCY: How to Get It, the Benefits & the Basic Rundown
https://www.youtube.com/watch?v=EjYmpVwAjKU

Ways to INSTANTLY Align with the Energy of Money & Abundance | Powerful Law of Attraction Secrets
https://www.youtube.com/watch?v=bHs7dgLXWIc

This Visualization Attracts Money! (Notice More Abundance Within 7 Days!)
https://www.youtube.com/watch?v=CPv1XtB3EQU

TOP AUDIOS TO LISTEN TO

https://www.thebutterflyeffectplanner.com/podcast

Printed in the United States of America

First Edition

Interior Design: Staci Weber Front & Back Cover: Staci Weber with template from https://www.fiverr.com/kozakura

Proofreader & Editor: https://www.fiverr.com/navywriter

ISBN-13: 978-1-7347082-2-6

www.jfbrou.com

www.ingramcontent.com/pod-product-compliance
Lightning Source LLC
LaVergne TN
LVHW081253100826
845148LV00009B/1216
9781734708226